12·14·79

DOKTOR BEY'S
BOOK OF
BRATS

WITH TEXT & COLLAGES BY DEREK PELL

AVON BOOKS
▲ PUBLISHERS OF BARD, CAMELOT AND DISCUS BOOKS

*DOKTOR BEY'S BOOK OF BRATS is an original
publication of Avon Books. This work has
never before appeared in book form.*

AVON BOOKS
A division of The Hearst Corporation
959 Eighth Avenue
New York, New York 10019
Copyright © 1979 by Derek Pell
Published by arrangement with the author
Library of Congress Catalog Card Number: 79-51350
ISBN: 0-380-46425-x

First Avon Printing, September, 1979

*AVON TRADEMARK REG. U.S. PAT. OFF. AND IN OTHER
COUNTRIES, MARCA REGISTRADA, HECHO EN U.S.A.*

Printed in U.S.A.

Jacket and book design by Louise Fili

FOR RON BERNSTEIN

CRADLE OF CONTENTS

As a lifelong student of *bratology*, I offer here the first illustrated dissection of that which plagues all intelligent men and women the world over: *the brat.* Be it called pest, punk, twerp, tot, tyke, rug rat, wart, whelp, waif, sapling, bastard, or bug...we know it for what it is: an *infernal menace* to the human race! The brat is the rotten apple in our barrel, the black sheep amongst our flock, the thorn in our side, the tack on our chair, the blemish at the end of our snout; it is the disturbing thunder in our sleep, the rain on our picnic, the unexpected snakebite, and the savage sneak attack! Yes, these drooling, dribbling, giggling little monsters are *everywhere*, crouched in constant conspiracy, crawling through the mud, whispering obscenities behind our backs!

Over the years a number of modest tracts have appeared in the form of anonymous pamphlets, with such titles as *Nursery Crimes, The Dreadful Load,** and *The Death of Silence As We Know It.* Though their purpose was clear and in concert, the authors of these papers failed to rise above their shrill, alarmist prose to achieve a dispassionate diagnosis of the Universal Threat.

Surely it is not enough to momentarily arouse the populace to random acts of punishment; for what *is* needed is a plan of concentrated action, coupled with continued intercourse between all members of the community and government whereby official guidelines are agreed upon. Furthermore, I advocate an international alliance which would provide for the return of runaways to the countries of their origin for public prosecution.

However, before we can properly and effectively

Based on an editorial in The London Widow's Walk *entitled "Pity the Pregnant? The Case For* Ostracism!" *(volume X, number VII, May 16, 1832).*

organize ourselves, we must look closely at the problem with a calm eye. This book marks the first step in that direction. Here contained is a plethora of information, a visual encyclopedia in rational format designed to provoke the sort of unemotional, yet *committed*, debate which will lead to an eventual solution.

When the reader has completed this introductory volume he will indeed "know thy enemy" from head to toe—his tricks, traits, and tactics. In addition, the reader will be better equipped to defend himself. The problem facing us will not simply crawl away should we beg our Creator, nor seek shelter high atop a mountain in Tibet. No, we must stand firm with strap in hand to meet this challenge, for today these creatures threaten to destroy our way of life. They brazenly boast ignoble deeds, taunt their teachers with sinful tongues, and make hostage their parents with threats of holding their breath until they "turn blue." To which I say, *let them*!

And may all our consciences be clear.

DOKTOR BEY
Barfmoor, England
6 February 1899

CHAPTER I
BASIC ANATOMY

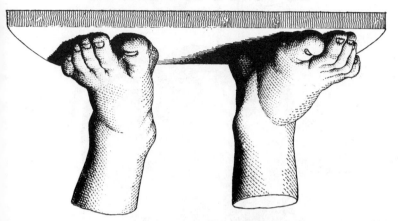

I'm afraid you've got a bad egg, Mr. Jones!
Oh no, my Lord, I assure you!
Parts of it are excellent!

William Pulteney, Earl of Bath

A WARNING TO THE READER:

Those of a squeamish nature or weak constitution may wish to proceed directly to Chapter II, for what follows is, indeed, gruesome and upsetting. I myself, while researching this section, became violently ill and, had I not been deeply in debt, would have abandoned this book altogether.

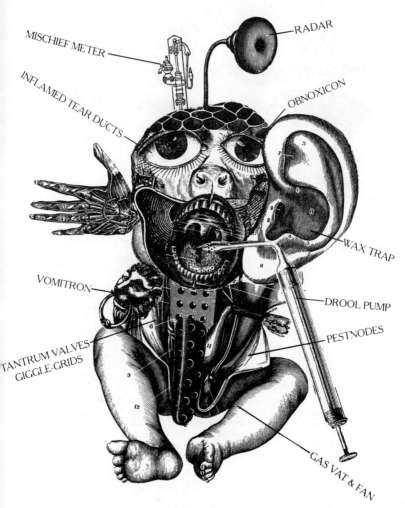

RADAR

MISCHIEF METER

OBNOXICON

INFLAMED TEAR DUCTS

WAX TRAP

VOMITRON

DROOL PUMP

PESTNODES

TANTRUM VALVES
GIGGLE-GRIDS

GAS VAT & FAN

AN INSIDE VIEW

*A cursory glance at the illustration above proves, once and for all,
that there can be no confusing the brat with the ordinary child.
The former comes equipped with so many indecent features and
accessories that it would be impossible for it to go undetected. It is as
if the Devil himself had set out to customize the little changeling,
implanting the viscid vomitron atop the toxic tantrum valves,
inserting the grotesque giggle-grids, the detestable drool pump,
and those wicked wax traps.*

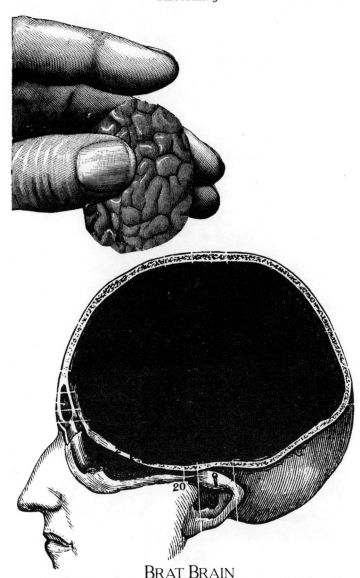

BRAT BRAIN

Though insignificant in size, the brain of a brat holds the key to the organism's misbehavior. The brain itself is compact, removable, and may be exchanged with the following three types: (a) monkey, (b) criminal, (c) walnut. In many cases the brain is taken out and never replaced.

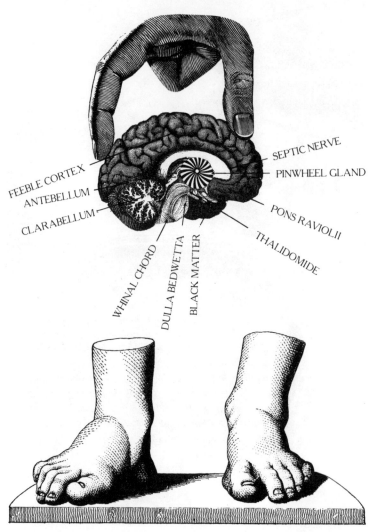

FEEBLE CORTEX
ANTEBELLUM
CLARABELLUM
SEPTIC NERVE
PINWHEEL GLAND
PONS RAVIOLII
THALIDOMIDE
WHINAL CHORD
DULLA BEDWETTA
BLACK MATTER

FEET

You can always tell a brat by its feet (most choose to go barefoot anyhow); the swollen ankles, bulbosity of toe, and unmistakable odor caused by a condition known as bastard's foot. The grotesque structural shape makes walking difficult and this is perhaps why many prefer to crawl (see page 38).

WARNING: A BRAT'S FOOT BRINGS BAD LUCK.

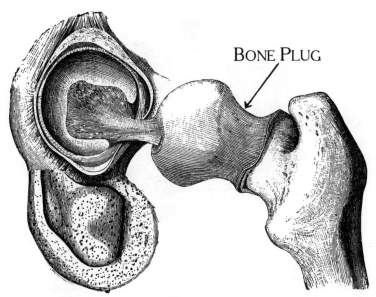

BONE PLUG

EARS

For those unfamiliar with brat anatomy it may seem strange that our Creator endowed the little pests with ears at all, since they are incapable of hearing adults. But why then have they no problems when amongst themselves? Because they are equipped with two inner bone plugs which enable them to block out intelligent conversation by simply gritting their teeth. Also, these plugs permit the brat to make maximum noise with minimum damage to itself. Brat ears are usually oversized,* ugly, and serve to store up large quantities of wax.

*Handy for pulling.

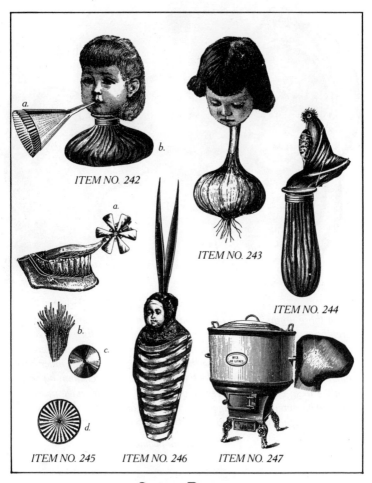

ITEM NO. 242

ITEM NO. 243

ITEM NO. 244

ITEM NO. 245   ITEM NO. 246   ITEM NO. 247

SPARE PARTS

No. 242 (a) Spit plug   (b) Sincerity simulator
No. 243 Pout sac
No. 244 Bladder pouch w/party hat
No. 245 Tongue Adaptors
No. 246 Antennae
No. 247 Snot Closet

FOR ADDITIONAL ACCESSORIES & INFORMATION
ON ORDERING SEE APPENDIX (PAGE 147)

DOKTOR BEY'S PICTORIAL PUZZLE PAGE

*See if you can find all 241 brats
hidden in this picture. Happy hunting!*

CHAPTER II
GESTATION

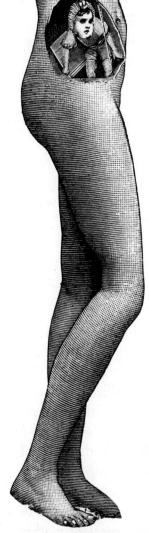

That is the true beginning of our end.

William Shakespeare
A Midsummer Night's Dream

To bring a brat into the world is not merely a selfish and irresponsible act, but a *declaration of war*; for here the progenitors *attack* the unarmed peace-and-quiet-loving population with a *sneak*. We must, however, bear in mind that the fornicator (man or woman) never knows *for certain*, until after the fact, if a brat is in the deck. A deadlier gamble I know not. Yet fate has a way of dealing out devils to those who either once were brats themselves or who have committed sins of equal magnitude.

Unfortunately, there is no written law that protects the rest of us from breeding mistakes as well. "But Doktor," you ask, "is there no way for us to prevent an awful offspring springing forth?" There is but òne route that is safe, which I recommend to all. Live alone, never address* the opposite sex, and dedicate all leisure hours to the composition of sonnets. Call it, *brat control.*

LADY-IN-WAITING OR EXPECTANT MOTHER?

At the outset a married woman must ask herself the question, *am I expecting*? If affirmative, she immediately qualifies as a common *housewife* (the *bitter half*). Should she, however, be intelligent enough to know precisely *what* she is expecting (either parcel, blizzard, or house-guest) then she is reclassified a *lady-in-waiting*.

Where's the rub? Here. Should she be deemed pregnant by a reputable physician (or impregnated by his disreputable counterpart), she becomes what is known as an *expectant mother.*† This is a condition characterised by nine months of extreme expectancy and other assorted syn-

*Nor undress. †For reactions to the news see chart, page 20.

dromes. Only at the termination of pregnancy does the woman learn what it is she has, for so long, been expecting: boy, or girl, or brat.

For the *expectant mother* who can not bear suspense (and most of them can't), she is advised to watch closely her own behavior for these signs of impending goon:

1. Severe state of melancholy throughout gestation.
2. Uncontrollable urge to stick out tongue at friends and relatives.
3. Repeated attempts at poisoning husband.
4. Successful attempt at self-destruction.

Please remember that these symptoms do not always result in the birth of a brat. She may simply be hysterical.

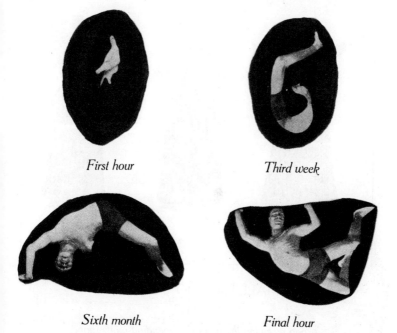

First hour   Third week

Sixth month   Final hour

POSITIONS & DEVELOPMENT OF BRAT IN THE WOMB

1. *Shock* 2. *Revulsion* 3. *Rage*

4. *Asininity* 5. *Dread* 6. *Self-Hate*

FEMALE EMOTIONAL CYCLE
CHART

Upon receiving the news of impending motherhood,
the wife experiences six distinct emotions.

THE MIDWIFE

A woman becomes increasingly repugnant during her months with brat, hence many husbands employ the services of a midwife who will act as a surrogate up until the moment of delivery. These lovely creatures enhance the passage of time during a man's most difficult period.

1. *Outrage*

2. *Revulsion*

3. *Despair*

4. *Expectancy**

*At the prospect of hiring a midwife.

MALE EMOTIONAL CYCLE
CHART
*Upon receiving the news of impending fatherhood,
the husband experiences four distinct emotions.*

THE WRITING ON THE WALL

*During the period of gestation some
women experience a certain scrawling
sensation which is terribly painful.
This is caused by an artistically
inclined foetus engaged in graffiti
(see Bohemian Brat, Chapter VI, page 71).*

A woman with brat *receives an injection of morphine, the most pleasant part of a painful operation.*

Some physicians advise placing the newborn brat in an incubustor *as a form of exorcism.*

TINKERING TRIPLETS

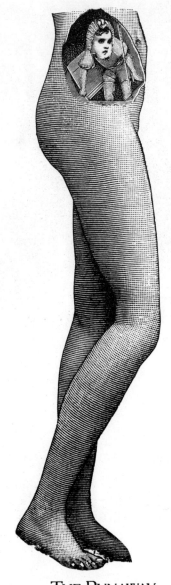

THE RUNAWAY

During the sixth month, brats have been known to attempt daring daylight escapes which prove highly embarrassing, if not fatal.

*Many physicians, called upon to deliver
a brat, will perform the operation under
a sheet so as to avoid fainting.*

At birth brats are not, as is customary with ordinary infants, "patted" on the bottom by the physician. Instead, they are dropped head first into an empty urn.

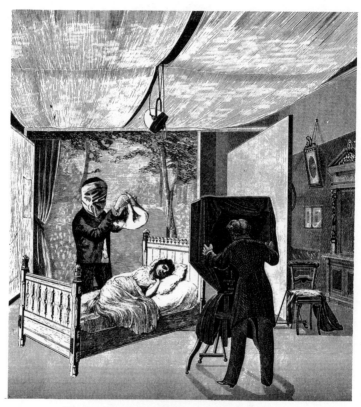

The husband who dabbles with daguerreotypes
*may wish to record the brat birth for
the purpose of blackmailing his wife.*

ANCIENT METHODS OF BRAT DELIVERY

1. Smoking the Bugger Out (Athens).
Patient was strapped to a table and placed over a bundle of burning fagots.

2. The Rack (France).
Patient was tied to a ladder made up of movable rungs, coerced into motherhood, and left with unsightly stretch marks.

3. Pop-Tut (Egypt).
Unequalled for ease and simplicity.

4. (Not Shown) Seesawian Section (Rome).
Patient was placed on the end of a long plank balanced by a central fulcrum. A heavy weight was then lowered onto the opposite end and quickly removed.

*WARNING: Should the above apparition
appear to you during gestation you will
give birth to twin brats and a dog!*

CHAPTER III

AFTER BIRTH

The wanton smiled, father wept;
Mother cried, baby lept.

Robert Greene
1580

While on a visit to a hospital in Leeds, I happened to overhear a woman, who had just unleashed upon us an overweight whelp, remark: "At least the worst part is done with." Her misconception enraged me. Had she been educated on the subject she would never have fornicated in the first place! Pushing a nurse out of the way, I stepped to her bedside.

"I beg your pardon, madam, but your *ignorance* compels me to comment. You are in for a *rude awakening!*"

"Oh, *am I?*" she sneered. "Then tell me sir, what could be worse than nine long months of torment?"

"Well, for starters," I said, "the next *two weeks!*"

I began to expound the horrors of brathood when I was rudely escorted from the room by two burly nurses.

How was I to know the women had a nervous condition?

The following chapter illustrates the point I failed to make that day in Leeds.

BREAST-FEEDING VS. VULTURE MILK

As preposterous as it may seem, some women are compelled to attempt breast-feeding two brats simultaneously, as if to kill two birds with one stone. This, however, is a highly dangerous and painful pursuit which may result in permanent disfigurement, if not humiliation. One alternative is the Tibetan Chest Protector (see Accessories); the other is to purchase gallon jugs of vulture milk and let the little buggers fend for themselves.
I have always been partial to the least encumbered approach,
but bear in mind the expense. 2075811

Although a mother may spend hours preparing her brat's meal, he will inevitably refuse to consume it. She is then expected to coax the little idiot with soft sounds and jabber. This too fails, after which the father is called upon to lend a steady hand, brute force, and an iron will. He may, after an hour or so, succeed— but to what end? The kitchen will appear as if it has been evacuated by an invading army while, a few minutes later, the dinner miraculously reappears.

THE RESULTS OF OVERFEEDING

FATHER OF THE BRAT

*It is customary, post partum, for the ordinary father to distribute cigars to his friends, while the man responsible for breeding a brat often flees to Havana and goes mad.**

**A sabbratical.*

There is no need to attempt teaching brats to walk
for they much prefer to snake, grovel, and roll.

1. *Deranged Infancy*   2. *Manic Mid-Life*   3. *Senility—Advanced*
(*thirteen weeks*).   (*twelve years*).   *State* (*thirty years*).

THE THREE CYCLES OF BRATHOOD
The brat who manages to survive his infancy and adolescent years will,
upon reaching the age of thirty, turn senile and acquire the physiognomy
of an antique.

HYGIENE TIPS N⁰ 36

BEWARE OF THOSE INNOCENT EYES!

I am often asked the following question: "Doktor, do brats breed disease?"—to which I respond with a resounding "you bet your tarboosh!" Indeed, these creatures are capable of carrying more than forty communicable diseases *simultaneously*. For evidence, we need only to turn to our history books. In 1348 much of Europe was devastated by the *bratbonic plague*,* which erupted prior to the invention of the airtight perambulator.

To be avoided at all costs are those brats with large blue eyes, for such deceptively innocent visual organs are the very means by which the brat transmits his germs. For those over thirty years of age, exposure to *brat-beams* for thirty seconds often proves fatal. Parents are here advised to blindfold all blue-eyed brats at birth, confine them to swaddling suits or armor, and pray for salvation.

*See *Archibald Rashblight's* The Brat Death, *Vector Editions, London, 1809.*

CHAPTER IV

NAMING THE BRAT

*Never...allow their names to
be mentioned in your hearing.*

Jane Austen
Pride and Prejudice

t the very least one would expect that the parents of a punk would take the time to label it accordingly, so as to alert the childless in advance. For example: to name a strange sapling *Jesus* is both blasphemous and misleading. What Christian soul would turn his back on little Jesus come to beg for sweetmeat? If, however, it were named *Hector* it would be instantly dispersed with an axe. The following list of names has been carefully selected to aid in the task of identification as well as provide the unimaginative with inspiration. Should any readers have suggestions of their own, please forward the names to the publisher with the utmost dispatch that they may be included in future editions.

MALE

Abortus	*Chatsworth*	*Fibster*	*Juggles*
Adolf	*Chauncy*	*Francis*	*Julian*
Alastair	*Clarence*	*Frelance*	*Junior*
Alphonso	*Cornelius*	*Fuster*	*Karl*
Barfolomew	*Crapwood*	*Gnatwood*	*Koddle*
Baltimore	*Cyrus*	*Hamilton*	*Kurdle*
Basil	*Derrick*	*Horace*	*Lambert*
Benito	*Dudley*	*Hubert*	*Louse*
Boris	*Dwight*	*Huckster*	*Leach*
Bruno	*Ebenezer*	*Ichabod*	*Leslie*
Bugwood	*Egbert*	*Idi*	*Leopold*
Cecil	*Ezra*	*Ivan*	*Llewelyn*
Cedric	*Fergus*	*Jerome*	*Lyman*

Maximilian	Phineas	Rollo	Vaguely
Monroe	Pierpont	Rupert	Vernon
Mugtar	Preymark	Silvester	Vincent
Mylar	Punkston	Snipper	Wesley ᴸ ᵃ ᴿ ᵘᵉ
Nigel	Queerlyle	Snotsy	Whinemore
Norbutt	Quentin	Staletto	Winston
Osgood	Raoul	Tarbud	Wolfgang
Padraic	Reginald	Tonto	Yasir
Percival	Roderick	Tut	Zigzag
Pestar	Rodney	Ubon	Zonk

FEMALE

Abigail	Frieda	Lymabina	Satanestra
Abortina	Futilda	Maude	Soupina
Alphonsine	Gangrina	Maybee	Spewella
Amelia	Geraldine	Mercedes	Steladora
Amonia	Germaime	Militint	Thorazine
Aurealia	Ghoula	Minerva	Trixandra
Babette	Gilda	Muella	Ukelele
Bayone	Godzila	Muriel	Vomitina
Bela	Harmonica	Murkey	Whorette
Blanche	Harpy	Myrtle	Wilhelmina
Bleache	Hashisha	Nabby	Winiford
Blobette	Hazel	Naomi	Yahula
Bordella	Hermione	Olga	Zitsy
Castraytina	Hildegarde	Opul	
Clorox	Hortense	Pamperina	
Cloysterina	Iceburg	Pestina	
Droola	Justine	Pigtalya	
Dunkette	Laverne	Pinchette	
Eva	Lizzie	Plethora	
Elmeretta	Lolita	Prudunce	
Eloise	Loadsa	Pukice	
Ernestine	Lorna	Purloina	
Eunice	Lotta	Quiksandra	
Fartella	Lopsy	Reba	
Faustina	Lulu	Roweena	
Forkdora	Luna	Ramoola	

CHAPTER V
COMMON TRAITS

The nursery lisps out in all they utter—
Besides, they always smell...

Lord Byron

host of loathsome characterological traits are ex-hibited by brats, everything from chronic knuckle-cracking to out-and-out *degeneration,* as if their physical presence were not bad enough! The average twerp comes complete with at least ten offensive attri-butes, yet others may exhibit hundreds *simultaneously!**

Here is a selection of the most common.

CONSTANT NOSE-PICKING

**Known in the trade as overkill.*

NAIL-BITING

JEALOUSY

MELANCHOLY

GREED

SADISM

CURIOSITY

MORBID CURIOSITY

PRECOCITY

DEGENERATION

POOR TABLE MANNERS

DOGMATISM

STUPIDITY

IMPROPRIETY

SAPLING RIVALRY

VANITY

POOR COMPLEXION

Close-up of skin condition

HOSTILITY

DOKTOR BEY'S
QUIZ BOX

A PENNY FOR YOUR THOUGHTS?

*Do not be fooled by what appears to
be two identical scenes between boy
and girl. One of these children is,
in fact, a brat. You must decide which
is the culprit and why. No hints.*

CHAPTER VI
COMMON TYPES

*They are born...and will please
themselves.*

Charles Dickens

When faced with the monumental chore of categorization, many bratologists have been driven to suicide.* This is understandable in light of the fact that there exists, crawling about the earth, some three thousand varieties. (I shudder to contemplate the consequences should life exist on other planets!)

With one or two exceptions, the brats in this chapter are within striking distance. They can daily be encountered in the city or, perhaps, on the farm. Yet how many of you can tell which is which? Who has not at one time or another erroneously cursed a *tombrat* as *guttersnipe*? But some will say what the devil difference does it make? To which I reply with the question: How can one adequately protect himself without knowing which whelp is assaulting him? And is it not important for the authorities to receive an accurate reporting concerning a crime? So there.

This section will also benefit the bewildered parent confused as to what particular model he or she has spawned. Is it fair for the father of a *sissy* to pay for the *vampire's* tantrum? Perhaps, but knowledge is power and power is truth and truth is justice.... 😈😈😈😈😈😈😈😈

*See Doctor Bey's Suicide Guidebook.

THE SPOILED BRAT

*Perhaps the most common type, the spoiled brat, is often associated with
the Upper Class and can be identified at birth by the protrusion of a silver
spoon from its mouth. After the first few weeks of life, this creature presents
its pater with a list of non-negotiable demands: (a) a steep allowance in
addition to a percentage of the gross family income, (b) a private
bedroom with access to the attic, (c) a pet boa constrictor, and (d) a pardon
all punishment for acts as yet uncommitted. Furthermore, should any of the
demands not be met, the child threatens to sully the family name
by entering politics.*

Spoiled brat burning his allowance.

SOILED BRAT
*Will, upon each and every minor spill,
demand a new wardrobe.*

UPSIDE-DOWN BRAT
(also "Show-off" or "Totsyturvy")

THE TOMBRAT

*Sometimes called a "feminist," the tombrat
is a strange creature indeed. Unlike most
little girls she refuses to play with dolls
and demands that her parents buy her a set
of barbells. At an early age her muscular
development is quite extraordinary and she
spends an inordinate amount of time climb-
ing trees. Like her male counterpart the
bully, the tombrat enjoys the art of fisti-
cuffs and favors the "surprise attack."*

BULLY
*Picks on those twice his size
(usually adults).*

SISSY
Constant companion to the bully.

FAT BRAT

*Consumes everything in sight including house-
plants, pets, and—occasionally—domestics.*

Sample of Brat Artistry

BOHEMIAN BRAT

Often artistically inclined, the bohemian brat prefers
symbolist poetry at bedtime, as well as a companion.

PATRIOTIK OR "BIRCH" BRAT
Often incites neighborhood children to oust by force all strangers suspected of abnormal sexual practises.

MATHEMATICAL BRATS
Adept at multiplying their family's misfortunes.

TATTLETALE
*Extremely dangerous when found in a household
whose patriarch has an eye for the ladies.*

BRATWURST
*Common in Germany. Characterized by
repeated attempts to invade Poland.*

VAMPIRE BRAT
*The only brat not known to nap but, instead,
sleep all day. Prefers blood to Mamma's milk.*

SATANIC BRAT
Generally named "Hellwood" or "Devilton,"
the satanic brat is recognizable at birth
by a pitchfork in place of a tongue.

GUTTERBRATS

SEA URCHINS
("Great White Waif")
*Travel out of schools and claimed responsible for
the decline in popularity of coastal resorts.*

BEACH BRATS
Aid and abet sea urchins

Were known in medieval Europe as "serfers."

POISON OAF

In recent years the bratologist has joined forces with the botanist in the naming of hazardous plants (totology). The results of their cross-pollination have produced the following: poison oaf, elfodil, spitunia, punkweed, rascalia, waifwort, milkwhelp, suckledud, and ragamuffin-weed. Admittedly, the totologist has a long way to go.

MASKED BRATS

*Unlike common criminals masked brats, upon returning
to their hideouts, do not remove their masks.*

CHAPTER VII
UNNATURAL HABITS

Knowest the mischief done!

Sir Isaac Newton

The brat's life is epitomized by its dedication to the pursuit of *pranks, naps,* and *games.* Often these three unnatural habits overlap. A game may be a prank and vice versa. The game may involve a nap which results in a prank. And a prank may lapse into dangerous sport that is followed by a nap. Or a nap may be merely a trick (which is part of a game and/or prank) to trap another unwary prankster in the act of nap so as to make him the butt of prank.

THE PRANK

It should be obvious to all but the feebleminded that a brat without a prank is as The Ripper without a knife. Despite their innate talent for lethargy, brats possess a bottomless pit of nervous energy which, each day, manifests itself in an eruption of obstreperous evil. Although stupid at school, when it comes to devising unusually cruel pranks the brat is a genius. The purpose of the prank is twofold: to humiliate their peers (for the sheer fun of it) and to reduce all responsible adults to babbling morons. Only the person who has never suffered the slingshots and arrows of outrageous brathood could dismiss a prank as "harmless" or excuse the activity by saying "boys will be boys."

Brats about to perform an unspeakable gang-prank.

POISONING SWANS

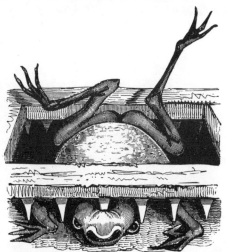

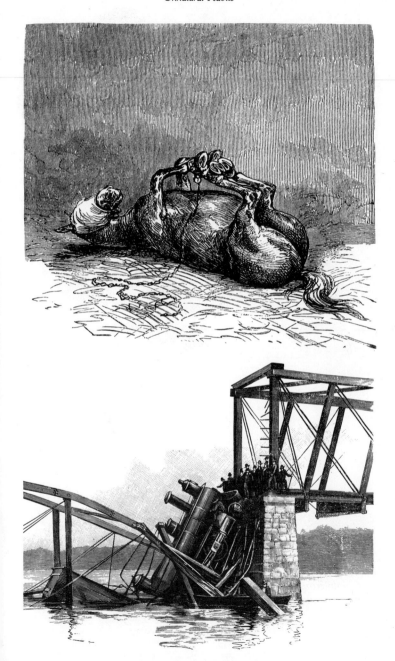

THE TANTRUM

*All brats are given to periodic, if not incessant, outbursts of bad
temper known as tantrums. This trait can actually be traced
back to 563 B.C. when in India a fat brat (see page 70) named
Buddha [Sanskratch = the obnoxious one] awoke from a brat nap
(see page 87) and began spitting violently, screaming, and
banging his head against a tree. This bizarre display of bile went
uninterrupted for nearly four years until, finally, he was struck
by enlightning and burned to a crisp. Unfortunately, Buddha's sacred
tantra* was handed down, brat by brat, and rapidly
spread to the West.*

**Secret recipe for throwing tantrum.*

THE BRAT NAP
("The Snooze of Satan")

*This strange phenomenon occurs at intervals throughout the day
(often at mealtime), when these slothful creatures fall into a trance
and are believed to commune with the Devil* himself. Some
brats manage this eerie "nap" while standing erect, while others
simply slump to the ground during chores.*

*Aggregate brats have been known to engage in grotesque
gang-naps, the sight (and sound) of which has driven many
a schoolmistress mad.*

*See *Satanic Brat,* page 74.

PLAYING HOUSE
This game develops skills in illegal entry and kidnapping.

PLAYING BARBER
*Often leads to another game
called "Brat the Ripper."*

PLAYING DOKTOR
Reinforces the brat's morbid curiosity.

Other brat games include:

Poke the Eye Out
Blind Man's Tough Luck
Squash
Craps
Polio
Water Polio
Mamma's Ring Toss
Pin the Tale on Nanny
Hot Poker
Twit Poker
Strap Poker
Strip Poker

Tar and Feathers
Trip Trap Foe
Ignite the Ragman
Tattle Bull
Hide the Piano
Baby On the Ledge
Robbing the Cradle
Robbing the Grave
Mortician
Mary-Go-Down-the-Well
Nursery Darts
Shoving Off

CHAPTER VIII

FUNCTION & UTILITY

LIVING OFF THE BRAT OF THE LAND

What on earth is the use of them?

Oscar Wilde

dults possessing a large stock of brat-o'-nine-tails and gifted in the art of intimidation may be able to put their whelps to good use. This approach (known as *turning the cradle to one's advantage*) can be applied in two areas: Sports and Slave Labor. The former includes public displays for profit as well as private amusements, while the latter remains the most practical application. Sending a pair of naked brats out into the gutter to beg can be richly rewarding for those who prefer idleness to employment. Brats can be especially profitable during blizzards at Christmastime when many adults, bereft of their senses, display charity as casually as a damsel will blush. So, too, can brats be forced to do all the unpleasant tasks which make life unbearable, i.e., sweeping chimneys, shoveling sewage, and erecting private mausoleums.

This chapter should provide a ray of hope for readers who, at this stage, are submerged in total despair.

A brat may be used to christen a ship.

ARMREST

PREY

BAIT

LEAP-BRAT

SPORTS

GUINEA PIG

CURIO

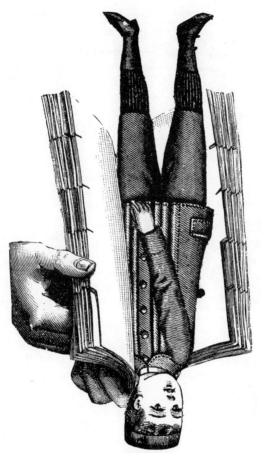

BOOKMARK

THE BULLYFIGHT

This exotic sport is slowly gaining ground in Great Britain.
Involves a man with cape and humorous costume (the bratador)
humiliating a neighborhood bully.

SPARRING PARTNER

CHAPTER IX

DISPOSAL

*If I do lose thee, I do lose a thing
That none but fools would keep.*

William Shakespeare
Measure for Measure

To dispose of unwanted brats (*punk-dumping**) presents the parent or guardian with a number of practical problems. Firstly, one must answer the obvious questions: (a) *How* doth I dispose of it? and (b) *Where* doth I dispose of it? Anyone who asks the question "Why?" should travel immediately to the nearest asylum.

Then there are those with large families who face the difficult choice between *mass disposal* or the *one-at-a-time* technique. If the latter approach is selected, the concern becomes: "Which one doth I dump *first*?" Furthermore, can the male brat be gotten rid of without his sister finding out and seeking revenge? Or vice versa.

Such dilemmas drive many would-be *punk-dumpers* to despair. Some lock themselves in closets in what is known as the "I'll-wait-till-they-run-away" syndrome. This is a cowardly corner for any adult worth his or her grey hair to be trapped into, for forget not this: THE RUNAWAY BRAT ALWAYS RETURNS! The act of *running away from home* is merely a villainous prank designed to torment. The mother and father, thrilled at the sight of their dangerous dwarf walking out the door, belongings in hand, later suffer the severe mental shock at the terrible tyke's return (the *heartless homecoming;* usually a few hours later, just when peace and quiet has settled in).

Needless to say, a brat will rarely dispose of itself, unless by sheer accident such as when playing with firearms.

By nature, brats will not "go peacefully" *anywhere*; why then should we expect them to *dance to their doom*?

*Not to be confused with punk-dunking.

They would much prefer to dance on *your* grave. Remember, time is on their side.

A twerp who gets wind of "the plot" will fight fang and nail to remain at home. Just as an insect refuses to depart from the fruit bowl for the open window, a brat will cling to his crib for dear life, rather than visit a relative in Tibet.

But I do not mean to leave the impression that disposal is impossible. Far from it; yet one must be clever. This chapter will give one courage as well as ideas.☺☺☺☺☺

AFTER THE QUAKE.
Nature can sometimes offer up surprising solutions!

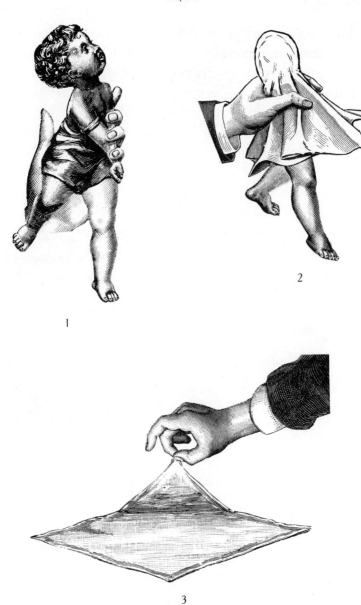

1

2

3

*Though expensive, one may wish to hire The Great Pudozo
to perform his famous disappearing brat trick.*

SUFFOCATION*

*Most effective at nap time or when
the brat is self-absorbed in a mirror.*

**Also called "smothering the tot with glove."*

Beware: brats have an uncanny knack for survival.

Nothing is fool-proof.

They will often turn up where least expected...

QUIZ BOX

PUT ON YOUR THINKING CAPS

When abandoning a brat, the parent is confronted with the question, "Where should I leave it?" A number of possibilities present themselves, some less effective than others. Let us test your resourcefulness. Choose two of the most propitious from the following list.

> *(a.) A neighbor's doorstep.*
> *(b.) Railway tracks in the next county.*
> *(c.) The cellar.*
> *(d.) A coal shaft.*
> *(e.) Scotland Yard.*
> *(f.) A political rally.*
> *(g.) In-law's outhouse.*

CHAPTER X

A Nanny's Manual

…a constant succession of disappointments.

Dr. Samuel Johnson

NOTICE FROM THE PUBLISHER:

The material contained in this chapter has been excerpted from an earlier work by the author, entitled The Art of Governing *(1883), which appeared under the pseudonym of Benjamin Gay, M.D. and was limited to one thousand copies, all given away by the printer. This edition has since become rare and is actively sought by bibulous collectors. Therefore, we are pleased to announce that several hundred damaged* dust jackets from the original volume have come into our possession, which we here make available to the readers of this book for a most-reasonable sum of 75p per wrapper.*

*Each spine severed at the edges, a few age stains, faint aroma, and water marks which, though of interesting design, obscure both woodcut and title on front. Otherwise mint.

INTRODUCTION TO THE ART OF GOVERNING

I n an age when English ragamuffins wreak havoc in the home and, by so doing, weaken the very foundations of the Empire, the role of the *governess* in Society can not be underestimated. Nay, these hard-bitten females we have come to call *nannies,* as well as the few effeminate men who have joined their ranks *(ninnies),* perform their distasteful duties bravely in the face of overwhelming *menace.* Rarely are they employed to contain a single dwarf, but instead must do battle with two, three, four, or more of these *pestiferous miscreants!*—since so many parents seem compelled to compound their errors! I recently read an account in the newspaper of a gentleman in Derbyshire who, while about his morning constitutional was surrounded by a pack of *thirteen* runts and publicly forced to disrobe! Later, when the local authorities rounded up these savage wrongdoers, it was discovered that *all* resided under one roof! The nanny of the house had, previously, been missing for over a month and has yet to be found.

Today, the Victorian governess is subjected to painful attacks on her person, vicious verbal assaults, amphibious invasions of privacy, and diurnal pranks of a perverse nature designed to drive her screaming from the grounds of the estate. Therefore it should come as no surprise to learn that, according to a recent survey conducted at Oxford, of those who survived their terms of employment as "louse-keepers," *seventy-two percent* required permanent confinement in a lunatic asylum. The other twenty-eight percent had fallen prey to self-murder. My own experience seems to confirm these findings as relates to the majority, for during a brief incarceration at the Bethlem Royal Hospital,* I discovered, to my dismay, that the entire population of patients (428), with the exception of two ex-M.P.s and myself, was comprised of mad nannies. That discovery prompted me to begin the research which has resulted in this book.

In view of such grim statistics one must inquire as to what motivates a woman of adequate, though uninspired, intellect to seek the position in the first place?

The answer is simple: the *salary.*

A wealthy patriarch is more than willing to divide his fortune with a lady who can guarantee him the luxury of uninterrupted leisure. Indeed, what chap worth his salt would not *cut off an arm* at the prospect of hardly ever having to lay eyes on the tiny thugs for, at least, the next ten years?! So too will the nanny gain from a mother who, equally elated (if not more so), showers her savior with jewels and expensive gowns in the thrill of abandoning responsibility. No more will she have to wean, tame, prune, or whack the ugly punklings—nanny has arrived!

Further, one must consider that the alternative to employment as governess is, most often, raising a family of one's own. 𝔊𝔊𝔊𝔊𝔊𝔊𝔊𝔊𝔊𝔊𝔊𝔊𝔊𝔊𝔊𝔊𝔊 𝔊

*Known unofficially as Bedlam.

SELF-DEFENCE

Due to the wide variety of brats a governess encounters, a thorough education in all known forms of self-defence is highly recommended. This should include everything from the ancient Japanese art of *jujitsu* ("tot-chopping") to the less graceful, but effective, American form known as *street-fighting* ("moppet-mugging"). It is no longer necessary to travel the world to acquire the secrets of self-defence; instead, one need only to enroll in the recently established *Nottingham School for Nannies.* ℚ

THE NOTTINGHAM SCHOOL FOR NANNIES
Motto: Self-Defence Is Our Highest Priority

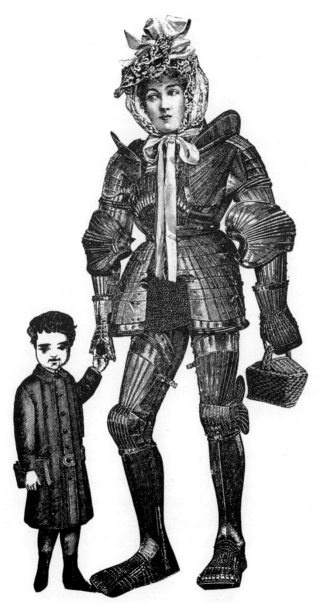

NANNY IN SHINING ARMOR
The latest in brat-protection, the suit of armor is once again practical (and fashionable as well!). May be worn on outdoor picnics or in the nursery.

TEN POINT PROGRAM/SUMMARY
from THE ART OF GOVERNING

1. THE INTERVIEW: Remember, first impressions are *essential* to your hiring. When greeting the prospective employer, never smile, appear faint, or feign coyness. Your speech should be sprinkled with obscenities. Appear *tough.* Be sure to *accurately* assess the patriarch's wealth, divide by two and, in no uncertain terms, announce your percentage. As well, it is advisable to request a reference in advance so as not to delay your future departure.

2. MEETING THE MONSTERS: *Wear your armor.* Show no emotion. To establish "upper hand" when brats are in assembly line, *swagger* over and deliver a single blow (full fist) to all. Remember, you have practised beforehand to assure maximum force and grace. If brats are spread about the room (crouching, on furniture, etc.) remain at the side of your employer, *do not turn your back to them*, but simply point an acknowledging lance in the direction of each.

3. LAYING DOWN THE LAW: Once hired, you will have been given free reign of the estate with exception of the barricaded area behind which reside your employers. Immediately proceed to place your illustrated punishment posters in a prominent place in each room (outside too).

4. FIRST AID: No matter how distasteful, it is essential to establish *immediate romantic link* with *largest* and most *fearsome* domestic and/or groundskeeper (preferably a gardener of Italian descent prone to violence) *on the premises* (servants from neighboring estates will not hear your cries for help).

5. NARCOTICS: Be sure your supply is adequate.

6. HEALTH—OR ELSE! Never allow your frequent depressions to keep you from eating and sleeping. Remember, once you have succumbed to illness and are bedridden you are entirely *helpless*!

7. REVERSE INTIMIDATION: On weekly basis make it a point to falsely accuse brats of *fabricated* crimes.

8. RETRIBUTION/OVERKILL: Your motto: "When one is guilty all must be punished." Remember to deliver a different punishment to each brat *separately* making certain the others bare witness. Most importantly, the penalty must *never* fit the crime but, instead, should *exceed* it in heinousness *fivefold.*

9. INFANTICIDE: Carefully measure your chances for success. While you should, of course, act fast, it is *mandatory* that you act *first.*

10. THE TRIAL: Remember to bring the portrait (or portraits) of the brat.

METHODS OF TRANSPORT

The transporting of brats can be awkward, embarrassing, and dangerous. I recommend first "drugging-the-bugger" with morphine which will aid in making travel both safe and discreet. Unfortunately, many brats refuse to "take the medicine," claiming not to be ill. If this is the case, then the drug may be taken by the transporter (no sense wasting good morphine) and though it will not make the mission any safer, it will certainly make it painless.

1

2

3

4

7

8

CRACKED BRAT
*CAUTION: Improper transport may result in the
formation of a cracked brat with homicidal tendency.*

PUNISHMENT

THE SLOPSINK
*Under the guise of toilet training, this ingenious
nursemaid has discovered a perfect punishment.*

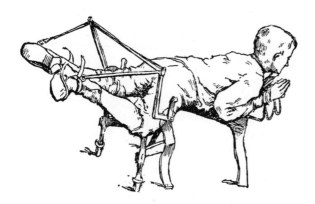

The Brat Rack

Dunking

CHAPTER XI
A BRIEF, SPORADIC HISTORY

L'histoire n'est que le tableau des crimes et des malheurs.
Voltaire

complete history of the brat, chronicling all the major misdeeds and mayhem from the beginning of time to the present, would require many years of research and would fill several volumes. My advanced years prohibit such a task and I leave the job to a much younger man who wishes to make his smudge among scholars. Instead, I have chosen to focus on some of the historical lowlights, not excluding the mythological links, which should provide the reader with, what I believe is, a serviceable overview.

EGYPTIAN BRAT BATH

According to The Papyrus of Ani (The Egyptian Book of the Brat) in the possession of the British Museum, a sacred brat bath was performed on the banks of the Nile. Bastards belonging to impeached Pharaohs were rounded up and dunked in the Great River in what was to have been a mass drowning in honor of Ra. Unfortunately Ptah-Nut was in a particularly foul mood that day and the brats, despite the heroic efforts of slaves, were graced with the power to float. As a result, three hundred buoyant brats drifted across the river to safety.

*Inspired by the ancient Egyptians, many parents
today pursue subtle variations of the brat bath.*

URCHIN'S CRUSADE
*In 1313, a band of scurfy urchins (armed with drums)
embarked from Marseilles and invaded Egypt. Led by young
Snipwood of Toyes, they conquered Cairo in three
days during a rampage unequalled in noise and destruction.*

GIANT VAMPIRE BRAT
PROWLS PHILADELPHIA!

The above headline appeared in the Philadelphia Sentinel *on
April 1, 1799. It was then and there that this curious legend began and,
despite the absence of reliable documentation, persists to this day.
Each year hundreds of tourists visit the "City of Brotherly Love"
hoping to catch a glimpse of the creature whom they call "Bracula".
Believed to be more than thirty feet tall (barefoot), "Bracula"
roams the streets in broad daylight searching for victims whose blood
it must drink to survive. Although the existence of vampire brats
is a well-established fact, it is doubtful that any such "giant" lives in
Philadelphia, the most boring of American cities.*

UFO

*Once again we must bow to the Colonies for both our superstition
and its definition. UFOs (Unidentified Flying Orphans) are said to be
inhabitants of neighboring planets who take to the air in strange
saucer-shaped craft and enjoy hovering outside windows and scaring
the daylights out of people. It is not surprising that the majority of
sightings occur along the Eastern Seaboard where the use
of opium is widespread.*

*In 1800, Eric Dreckwater, while vacationing
at a hotel in Barfmoor, ordered two brats
over-easy and, upon digesting them, succumbed
to the only recorded case of totulism.*

BRAT BUST

*London, 1802. One hundred and thirty-six punks were
brought into custody after authorities discovered
Miss Sylvia Prim, Head Mistress of Hanover Hall,
tied to the tracks at Victoria Station.*

Between the years 1851–1853, E. D. Davies, a drunkard from Boston, Massachusetts, is believed to have delivered some twelve thousand brats. His recent arrest and execution should serve as a warning to witch doctors everywhere.

*In 1830, Buster Cusp, while weeding his back-
yard, discovered the Tomb of the Unknown
Brat. This site, located in Peoria,
Illinois, draws tourists from around the globe.*

One of the more shameful episodes in brat history occurred in Coventry on November 16, 1852, when Lolita Wheatly, twelve-year-old daughter of Humbug and Hazel Wheatly (a deranged mason and seller of shells in winter, respectively), was apprehended and charged with the seduction of nine members of her own family, in addition to four domestics!

In true brat fashion, Lolita appeared at her trial dressed in a lion's suit to convey her utter contempt for our legal system. She was accompanied by one Sebastion K. Threwbrick, a lad of mere six who, upon entering the dock in her *defence*, poked the barrister in the eye with a pin and shouted: "*Now back off!*" Subsequently, the defen-

dant was declared guilty and invited to choose one of two punishments, i.e., death by jail, fire or public beheading. From within the dark of her costume, Lolita roared with laughter and began to waltz inventively about the court until a guard restrained her. The infuriated magistrate withdrew his unusually fair offer and, instead, sentenced the sinfully bent nymphet to spend the rest of her natural life confined to the company of an insufferable (stuffy) lepidopterist at his home in Montreux.

🐦 *Lolita Wheatly*

THE GREAT FINK'S ROBBERY ATTEMPT (1888)

Nearly successful at looting the Fink's Brothers Bank in London, the notorious "Baby-Faced Nelson" was thwarted by an alert dick.

THE STRANGE & CURIOUS CASE OF SISTER CARLOTTA

In 1857, at a nunnery north of Rome, Sister Carlotta Luccia Wyamea awoke one night from a troubled sleep. The mother superior arrived at her bedside and became quite concerned upon noticing an odd distention at the top of the young nun's habit. "And what is this, my child?" enquired the abbess who, patting the bulge, suspected contraband. "Don't touch it!" retorted Carlotta, pushing away the woman's hand. "It *hurts*." The abbess listened skeptically as the girl explained the nature of her discomfort as a series of "heavenly headaches" which had, for months, disturbed her slumber. Distressed by such talk, the mother

superior summoned a physician from the city. He arrived to discover the nun in great agony, rolling about the floor and mumbling incoherently. He commenced a rather lengthy examination (a fortnight) at the conclusion of which he announced a shocking diagnosis: "I am afraid you're suffering *with brat* in, of all places, the *cranium.*"

The mortified sister sat in silence as the doctor explained, "It is, for a woman of your position, better to *receive* than *give*. The results, you see, have gone to your head. In fact," he added, smiling, "one might say you've a brat in your belfry."

"*But that's impossible!*" protested the virgin, angrily. "Why, I haven't even *seen* a member of your sex for nearly *two years!*"

The physician was nonplussed. The abbess was outraged and immediately ordered the nun away with words that have since become legend.*

"Get thee from the nunnery!"

A month of arduous travel took our heroine to Paris where she appeared at the doorway of 110 Rue Morgue, the residence of the renowned Belgian bratologist Maurice Dildeaux. Noting with horror the young woman's condition, which in the interval had worsened considerably, Dr. Dildeaux invited her in and escorted her to his study. There she began to babble and weep until the physician comforted her with an injection. Calmly, she explained her ordeal and, at the conclusion, said: "You *must* believe me, Doctor...Do you?"

Dildeaux sat for a moment without speaking, his hand to his chin in contemplation. Removing a pen from the desk, he began marking down numbers on a small pad and counting on his fingers.

"What," he asked bluntly, "are your financial circumstances?"

Carlotta assured him of adequate compensation.

"Well, then," winked Dildeaux, "I'll accept your tale at face value."

The next several weeks were devoted to an intense investigation of the expectant skull, during which time the specialist consulted hundreds of tomes, pausing only for nourishment, waste disposal, and his daily dose of cocaine. Meanwhile, rumors had begun circulating round the city, and Carlotta had to be confined to the attic where, through the cracks of the boarded-up window, she observed a crowd of morbid curiosity-seekers.

As the day of delivery drew near Dildeaux was still without a *modus operandi*.

"It's going to be rough sailing," he told his patient, eyeing her ill-fitting wimple. Yet despite her macabre cranial proportions, he saw that Carlotta had quite a lovely figure (especially for a nun). For days a certain something had been brewing beneath his dispassionate exterior.

Finally, on the eve of the operation, Maurice and Carlotta sought solace in each other's arms:

"But," she whispered, "I feel so...so unclean."

"Leave on the headress."

The very next morning hundreds who had maintained an unruly vigil outside were still there, passing bottles of wine back and forth. Inside, Dildeaux looked to the heavens for guidance while Carlotta fainted. No answer was forthcoming so, undeterred, the doctor proceeded to improvise.

Fourteen hours elapsed before the physician emerged from the house looking exhausted and pale. He stepped into the crowd and announced the news of his patient's "immaculate cranial conception" and the subsequent successful bit of skulldiggery.

"I have performed a most *miraculous* surgery," he told them, "which, henceforth, will be known as a *lobratomy*!"

The crowd threw vegetables.

Wearing a plain brown sack over her head, Carlotta escaped by way of the back door. With the brat tucked beneath her habit she ran to a nearby orphanage where, for an outlandish fee, the disposal was transacted.

Carlotta Luccia Wyamea never saw her savior again for he expired at the hands of the mob. Her saga concluded in California where she settled the following year. There she publicly denounced her Catholicism and formed a cult of her own.

*The accessories displayed on the following pages
were chosen especially for readers of this book
from the more than two million items currently
listed in the catalogue from Doktor Bey's All-Night
Emporium. Should the reader wish to order two or more
of these fine products, he may simply send the
appropriate payment (Tibetans add one thousand £)
with your name and residence to Bey's Emporium,
16 Pickle Row Terrace, London, England. Be sure to
print clearly the item number for each product ordered.*

WHEN IN LONDON VISIT DOKTOR BEY'S ALL-NIGHT EMPORIUM
(LOCATED JUST 3 BLOCKS SOUTH OF VICTORIA STATION)

Staffed by hundreds of courteous, well-groomed gentlemen
of indeterminate age, whose only desire is to uncover a
satisfied customer of the opposite sex. Yes, *Doktor Bey's*

All-Night Emporium features only the finest products (over two million in stock!) for the discerning individual of independent means. Why not bring the entire family* and spend a day roaming among our spacious rows of unforgettable merchandise, imported from as far away as Fort Leavenworth (near the Santa Fe Trail in Kansas) and as nearby as Fleet Street. Choose from the many vats of International Conversation Pieces where you can pick up an Albanian Training Stool for half price, or an Egyptian toe-warmer, or even a mustache cup for two! The EMPORIUM also features a wide range of *contraband*, tastefully displayed in our Opium Room, adjacent to the highly popular Tower of Courtesans. And should you desire a bite to eat on your stroll through our warehouse (over ten kilometers wide!) it is just a hop, skip, and a jump to the Empire Snack Bar run by none other than the Doktor's own brother! That's correct, ladies and gentlemen, Ray Bey himself will be on hand to personally serve each and every one of you some of his own fish and chips dripping with a special sauce handed down to him by extinct relatives from Tibet. While you're at it, have a cup of tea on us! Just our way of saying *"c'est selon"* for exploring all the delights and surprises at *Doktor Bey's All-Night Emporium.* If lucky, you may even be invited to step into our Private Office where, with your own eyes, you can read from our files countless testimonials from around the globe, written by persons whose names, though difficult to spell, mean quality. So put down this book and make your way to *Doktor Bey's All-Night Emporium* (open all night every Wednesday) —the place where people like to meet, spend money, and misplace their personal effects.

Children not admitted unless wearing shackles.

ACCESSORIES

No. 461	BRAT-TATTOO KIT *(branding iron not included)*
No. 462	SILVER SPOON
No. 463	EMERGENCY TOTLINE *(direct to nearest constabulary)*
No. 464	BAMBINO TONGS
No. 465	BRATRILOQUIST DUMMY
No. 465½	TOM THUMB SCREW *(with room for pinkies too)*
No. 466	THRASH-MASTER *(spanks continuously for up to four hours)*
No. 467	DUNCE CAP *(quantity orders only)*
No. 470	SEEN-AND-NOT HEARD LIPCLAMP
No. 471	BRAT BEACH SUIT *(one size fits all)*
No. 472	CANDELABRAT
No. 473	IMMOBILE ICE SKATES *(great for Christmas)*
No. 474	HIGH-CHAIR
No. 475	HAITIAN HEX BUG *(out of stock)*
No. 476	BRAT CAP
No. 477	TIBETAN CHEST PROTECTOR
No. 478	DOKTOR BEY'S FOOLPROOF BRAT TRAP
No. 480	DOKTOR BEY'S BRAT INSURANCE

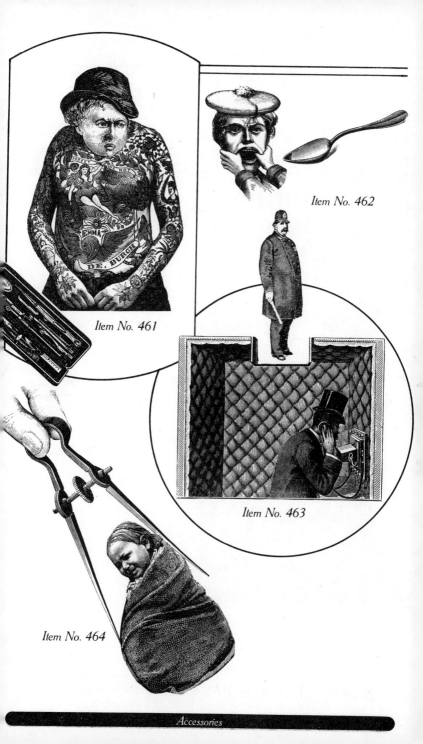

Item No. 461

Item No. 462

Item No. 463

Item No. 464

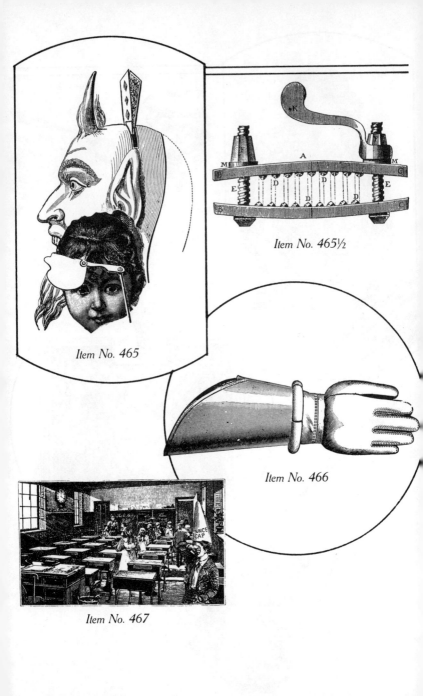

Item No. 465

Item No. 465½

Item No. 466

Item No. 467

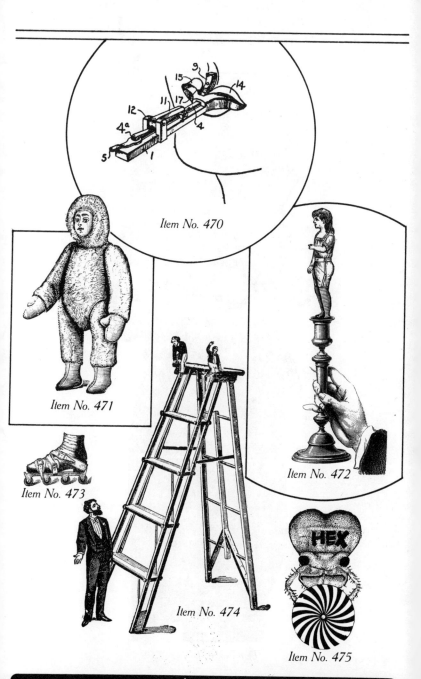

Item No. 470

Item No. 471

Item No. 472

Item No. 473

Item No. 474

Item No. 475

Item No. 476

Item No. 477

TIBETAN CHEST PROTECTOR

*Indispensable for maintaining a safe distance between milkmaid
and brat. Designed with an eye for Victorian fashion, the T.C.P.
may be worn out-of-doors or to the opera. It comes complete
with a sturdy apeskin harness, dual mammary-masks, and a
seven-inch safety tube (additional extensions are available for long
distance feeding of up to four kilometers).*

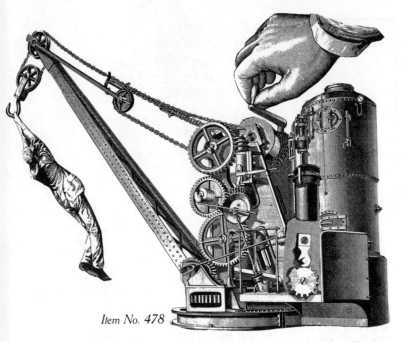

Item No. 478

Here is the invention you have all been waiting for, Doktor Bey's Foolproof Brat Trap, guaranteed to nip that nuisance in the bud! Just set trap near the infected area and wait for the results. For large families we recommend the purchase of one for every room. An attractive piece of furniture, the Brat Trap is suitable for any decor.

HOW IT WORKS

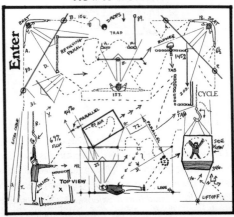

UNABLE TO SLEEP?
UNABLE TO THINK?
UNABLE TO SWALLOW?
CAN'T AFFORD TO HIRE A GOVERNESS?
DO YOU FEAR FOR YOUR LIFE?

RELAX!

Place your faith in the Doktor's safe.
Sign up for...

BEFORE

DOKTOR BEY'S

BRAT INSURANCE

FULL COVERAGE PROTECTS YOU AGAINST:

• LOSS OF HEARING DUE TO SUDDEN EXPLOSIONS •
• SNAKE BITES •
• BURNS THE RESULT OF HOT-FOOT •
• HAIR LOSS DURING SLEEP •
• DAMAGE TO THE SKIN CAUSED BY TAR •
• THEFT OF LIMB •
• SCRATCH MARKS •
• CIGAR BURNS •
• HEART FAILURE UPON ENTERING THE ATTIC •
BEDROOM
NURSERY
OUTHOUSE

For complete details and a
sample policy send your
name & address to:
DOKTOR BEY'S BRAT INSURANCE
c/o DOKTOR BEY'S ALL-NIGHT
EMPORIUM
16 Pickle Row Terrace

Act Now! It is later than you think.

A PARTIAL BIBLIOGRAPHY

LA PHILOSOPHIE DANS LE BRAT
Marquis de Sade

OXFORD BOOK OF ENGLISH BRATS

A BRAT'S CHRISTMAS IN WALES
Dylan McTilton

A THOUSAND AND ONE ARABIAN BRATS

PORTRAIT OF THE ARTIST AS A YOUNG BRAT
Randall Joyce

REMEMBRANCE OF BRATS PAST
Marcel Proust

BRATS AND PUNISHMENT
Fëdor Dostoevski

CONFESSIONS OF A BRAT
James Ricketts

THE BRATS IN MY LIFE
M. Hubbard

TWENTY THOUSAND BRATS UNDER THE SEA
Jules Verne

BRAT ANATOMY
Robert Burton

THE BRAT WITHOUT A COUNTRY
Edward Everett Hale

PORTRAIT OF A BRAT WITH RED HAIR
Hugh Walpole

THE INVISIBLE BRAT
H. G. Wells

BRATS IN BONDAGE
Count Salvator Lucci

THE JUNGLE BRAT
Rudyard Kipling

Portrait of the author being pestered by a brat.

Other books by Doktor Bey:

DOKTOR BEY'S SUICIDE GUIDEBOOK
(Dodd, Mead & Co., 1977)

DOKTOR BEY'S BEDSIDE BUG BOOK
(Harcourt Brace Jovanovich, 1978)

DOKTOR BEY'S HANDBOOK OF STRANGE SEX
(Avon Books, 1978)